BEST
BLENDER
RECIPES
EVER

BEST
BLENDER
RECIPES
EVER

FAST, HEALTHY RECIPES
TO WHIP UP FOR EVERY MEAL

REBECCA MILLER FFRENCH

PHOTOGRAPHY BY JUSTIN LANIER

THE COUNTRYMAN PRESS

A DIVISION OF W. W. NORTON & COMPANY

INDEPENDENT PUBLISHERS SINCE 1923

Copyright © 2016, 2015 by Rebecca Ffrench
Photographs copyright © Justin Lanier

Material previously published in *The Ultimate Blender Cookbook*

For information about permission to reproduce selections from this book, write to
Permissions, The Countryman Press, 500 Fifth Avenue, New York, NY 10110

For information about special discounts for bulk purchases, please contact
W. W. Norton Special Sales at specialsales@wwnorton.com or 800-233-4830

Library of Congress Cataloging-in-Publication Data

Names: Ffrench, Rebecca Miller, author. | Lanier, Justin, photographer (expression)
Title: Best blender recipes ever : fast, healthy recipes to whip up for every meal /
Rebecca Miller Ffrench ; photography by Justin Lanier.
Description: Woodstock, VT : Countryman Press, a division of W.W. Norton &
Company, [2016] | Series: Best ever | Includes index. Identifiers: LCCN 2016011930 |
ISBN 9781581573893 (pbk.)
Subjects: LCSH: Blenders (Cooking) | Smoothies (Beverages) | LCGFT: Cookbooks.
Classification: LCC TX840.B5 F47 2016 | DDC 641.5/893—dc23 LC record available at
https://lccn.loc.gov/2016011930

The Countryman Press
www.countrymanpress.com

A division of W. W. Norton & Company, Inc.,
500 Fifth Avenue, New York, NY 10110
www.wwnorton.com

10 9 8 7 6 5 4 3 2 1

TO MY FAMILY,
WHO LOVES A GOOD LAUGH
AND GREAT FOOD.

AND TO ALL BLENDER LOVERS
LOOKING TO WHIR THEIR WAY
TO WHOLESOME MEALS.

BEST BLENDER RECIPES EVER
CONTENTS

Introduction

While working on this book, I was often asked questions like, "Why the blender? Isn't it easier to mix things by hand? Don't you find it hard to clean?" The short answer: No.

The long answer: A blender can greatly assist a home cook with chopping vegetables, mixing marinades for main courses, and literally whipping up a wholesome dessert—all in minutes. A blender makes meal prep quick and easy. It's a helpful tool for turning fresh, local ingredients into healthful meals—and not just liquid ones. You can greatly boost your nutritional intake by adding greens, nuts, and superfoods to your diet on a daily basis. And the best part: Nutritious can equal delicious!

You see, from the third grade the blender was the one appliance that I didn't have to ask permission to use. I was free to create as I pleased. And so I did. And have continued to do so for almost 30 years, developing recipes that give bang for their buck—creative combinations of natural foods that are nutrient-dense, enhance energy, and, most important, come together quickly.

My first forays into blending involved lots of milk shakes and salsas—perfect after-school snacks for the tween years. During my college days, my blender was primarily an ice crusher (and probably saw more alcohol than it should have!). As I matured and got married, my blender took on a more sophisticated role, blending vinaigrettes and pureeing sauces.

Then baby made three and the blender worked tirelessly pulverizing vegetables into healthy, preservative-free mush for our new addition. Along came baby two, and life got even more hectic, but our blender did not give up on us, nor we on it. Its blades still whirred, now accommodating four. We whipped up everything seemingly possible in our blender: crêpes, muffins, meatless burgers, and more.

When the smoothie phenomenon hit, we were already there, blending away. I found ways to incorporate more foods rich in fiber, antioxidants, and heart-friendly fatty acids into every dish.

In these pages, I want to share my love of blending and show how this miraculous machine can effortlessly aid you in the quest for healthier eating. I admit, I'm a food fanatic. I obsess about every bite my family and I ingest. I want each morsel to melt in our mouths, leaving us happy and satisfied. I hope these recipes relay my sense of excitement about food: bright colors, juicy textures, diverse flavors.

Eating should make you feel good—physically *and* socially—and the blender can help get you there . . . fast. It minimizes prep time, allows you to easily make large quantities for a crowd, and truly is a cinch to clean.

You, too, can turn your blender into a kitchen workhorse, making meals a time to recharge, relax, and connect.

Healthy Made Simple

What is the key to successful blending? Fresh, wholesome ingredients. The fresher the produce, grain, nut, or other foodstuff, the truer the flavor and the more complete the nutrition. You are in control of every ingredient you put in the blender, so the result is up to you. You can replace store-bought foods like soups with homemade, chemical-free equivalents and swap syrupy bottled salad dressings for sugarless blends.

According to the Centers for Disease Control (CDC), only 32.5 percent of Americans eat the recommended two or more servings of fruits per day. The number drops even lower, to 26.3 percent, for those who eat the recommended three or more servings of vegetables per day.[*] That means a lot of us aren't eating our fruits and veggies!

Enter the blender. Large amounts of fruits and vegetables can be blended to manageable sizes for easy consumption, and the blender's blades break down cell walls of hard-to-digest raw plant-based foods for better absorption.

It may be tempting to load up drinks with sugar or sauces with cream, but there's no need when blending. Fruits lend sweetness while nuts and healthy oils can create velvety texture.

This collection of recipes may serve as a user manual for beginning blenders, a springboard for those looking to incorporate more fruits and vegetables in their diets, or a resource of new ideas for those already proficient with their blenders.

The goal with these recipes is to use the blender to its fullest potential. Its power is uncanny. A vortex is actually created inside the blender jar, which brings me to the second, third, and fourth most crucial elements of blending: Do not overblend, do not overblend, do not overblend. I know I'm being repetitive, but this should become your mantra. I will reiterate it throughout the book, but when a recipe says to pulse, really pulse. It's so tempting to go just a

[*] Centers for Disease Control and Prevention, "State-Specific Trends in Fruit and Vegetable Consumption Among Adults—United States, 2008–2009," *Morbidity and Morality Weekly Report* (September 10, 2010).

little more, but a few extra seconds of blending and a potato soup can go from satiny smooth to gummy glue. You can always blend more, but it's difficult to reverse the effects of overblending without starting over, so go slowly. Believe me, I've had to start again more than once (my dog is always happy to sop up my mistakes, though; she never seems to mind the texture!).

My hope is that this book helps make the blender your buddy, that you'll see it as an approachable assistant helping you prepare tasty, healthy meals. I also hope these recipes become part of your daily repertoire, essentials you love and go back to again and again. Use the blender to experiment, put good food on the table, and get things done fast, but most of all—have fun with it!

A Word About Blenders

I use a Vitamix Professional Series 750, and I *love* it. To me, it is the Bentley of blenders. I also have an Oster blender and the Ninja Ultima blender. They both do a fine job, but I have a difficult time blending up burgers in the Oster, and the Ninja just doesn't have the power of the Vitamix. Neither grinds nuts and seeds as thoroughly as the Vitamix.

The Blendtec and the Vitamix are extremely comparable. They both work well, it's just what bells and whistles you prefer. Take time to comparison shop and you'll find the right fit. Both will do an exceptional job.

That said, power blenders are extremely expensive. The payoff: healthy natural food prepared with little effort. Power blenders are built to last a lifetime. Most of the recipes in this book require a high-speed blender. Smoothies, salad dressings, and marinades will work with conventional blenders, but for those looking to blend up dishes for every meal, you'll need a power machine. Consider the money spent as an investment in your health, your future, your happiness.

CHAPTER ONE

BLENDER BASICS

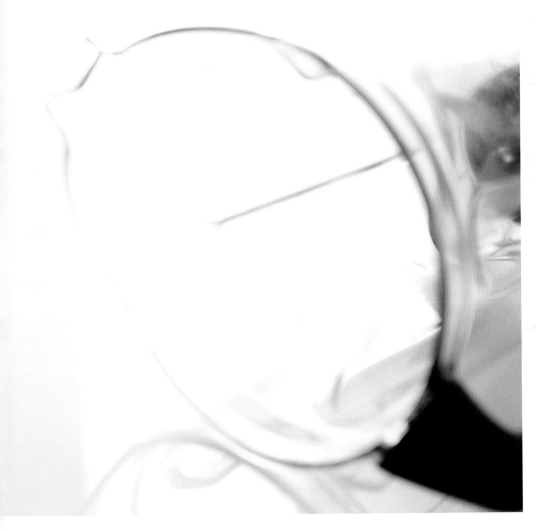

Are you ready to start blending? Incorporating blender recipes into your daily meal plan will make your life easier—and make you feel good too. But where to start?

The first step: Look at your own kitchen. What ingredients do you have on hand? Using the blender has inspired me to think differently about what I keep in my cupboards and fridge. I have slowly added new ingredients to my shelves—lots of seeds, nuts, and whole grains—and stocked my fridge with an array of fresh produce. The blender has inspired me to consume such a wider variety of fruits and vegetables than ever before.

There are also some important techniques to keep in mind when using a blender. Having a light touch and not over-blending is often the key to success. Remember to work with the blender, not against it. The blender does need your assistance sometimes—you're a team. Actually we're a team: you, me, and the blender. So let's get to it and start blending!

A Well-Stocked Blender Kitchen

Some of the ingredients in this book may be new to you—they were to me just a few years back. While my local market carries most ingredients used in this book, when I asked the cashier if they sold chia seeds, she melodically chimed back, "Ch-Ch-Ch-Chia? Aren't those sold on TV with a clay pet?" And even my own mother asked, "Can you get high from hemp seeds?"

Most of these items should be readily available at conventional markets, but you may have to search farther afield to find a natural food store or online retailer.

Budget is a huge consideration when stocking your cupboards with organic, natural staples. Healthy foods don't come cheaply, so slowly build up your pantry. Add oils, grains, sweeteners, and superfoods as you use them. No need to buy everything at once. Once purchased, a little does seem to go a long way. A good jar of raw honey can last months. Buying in bulk is another money-saving option. And save even the smallest amounts of ingredients. You never know, you may just need a teaspoon of almond flour tomorrow.

Essentials at a Glance

IN THE PANTRY

Oils cold-pressed extra-virgin olive oil, cold-pressed extra-virgin coconut oil, aroma-free coconut oil, organic canola or grapeseed oil

Vinegars balsamic, apple cider (Bragg's), white wine, red wine, and rice wine vinegars

Flours white whole wheat, spelt, oat, light buckwheat, almond, and coconut flours

Grains old-fashioned rolled oats, brown rice

Legumes lentils, chickpeas, black beans

Nuts and Seeds almonds, pecans, walnuts, cashews, flaxseeds, hemp seeds, pumpkin seeds, chia seeds, quinoa, nut butters

Sweeteners raw honey, maple syrup, dark brown sugar, organic cane sugar, confectioners' sugar

Canned goods coconut milk, fire-roasted tomatoes, artichoke hearts, beans, chipotles in adobe, pumpkin

Carton goods almond milk, organic chicken broth

Spices and such Maldon salt, kosher salt, cinnamon, coriander, cumin, ginger, nutmeg, paprika, red pepper flakes

Baking items baking powder, baking soda, pure vanilla extract, unsweetened cocoa powder, bittersweet chocolate chips, unsweetened coconut, dates, baking spray

IN THE FRIDGE

Organic eggs, butter, buttermilk, plain yogurt, ricotta cheese, lemons, limes, Dijon mustard, fresh herbs (cilantro, parsley, rosemary, thyme, basil), kale, and other leafy greens

IN THE FREEZER

Ice, homemade chicken stock, berries

IN THE PRODUCE BIN

Avocados, onions, garlic, shallots, fresh ginger

Tips & Tricks

LIQUIDS AND SOFT FOODS FIRST

How you load your blender may make a difference in your outcome, and keep things blending smoothly without extra spatula action. Add liquids and soft foods to the blender container first, then put the harder ingredients on top, including ice.

GO SLOWLY AND DON'T OVERPROCESS

I said it before and I'll say it again: *Do not* overblend. The blender is a powerful machine, and the consistency of something can go from great to ghastly in seconds. Just go slowly. Less is more.

When your machine is whirring with nothing moving inside, stop it and push the ingredients toward the blade with a spatula. I rarely expect that everything will blend up evenly without a little help from a spatula. It's good to make sure all the bits of what you're blending are out from under the blades and fully integrated.

Also go easy on your machine. When it gets overly warm or starts to sputter, turn it off and let it cool down.

NO NEED TO MINCE

A primary advantage to using a blender is ease. I purposefully call for large pieces of vegetables and cloves of garlic only cut in half once to avoid lots of time spent dicing and chopping. Let the blender do the work. There may be one or two recipes where you do have to mince, but only because, for example, only half the soup gets blended in order to retain texture; in this case the garlic should be minced since not all of it will be pureed.

EVERYTHING TO TASTE

Almost every recipe in this book calls for salt, pepper, or some other type of seasoning. Use the amounts listed as a guide, but don't hesitate to use more or less according to your preference.

Another beauty of blending is that unlike baking, it's not an exact science (that is, unless you're making something like blender brownies or a cake).

You can always add another squeeze of lime or sprig of cilantro and keep testing until the flavors seem balanced to you. If something tastes too sweet, add an acid; too sour, add a sweetener. Play around. Taste as you go.

EASY CLEANUP

The very best to way to clean your blender is to do it right away. Don't let food dry and harden inside the container. It only takes seconds to clean. Fill your blender about one-third full with hot water and a few drops of liquid dish soap. Place the lid on the blender, place the pitcher back on the base, and run it on low for a few seconds, then turn it to high for a minute. Pour out the water, rinse the blender with more hot water, and use a dish brush to scrub out any remaining food should there be any. That's it, your blender is clean!

SOAKING NUTS, SEEDS, GRAINS, AND LEGUMES

Lots of nuts, seeds, grains, and legumes are used in this book, and they all naturally contain phytic acid. Phytic acid binds to minerals and prevents them from being absorbed by our bodies. It's debatable whether phytates (phytic acid) should be of concern. However, to avoid them, you can soak nuts, seeds, grains, and legumes. Not only does soaking reduce phytic acid, it also neutralizes enzyme inhibitors that are present, which some say can cause trouble with digestion.

On a more functional level, soaking nuts makes them much easier to grind for nut milks. If you soak nuts before making nut butters, they must be thoroughly dried at a temperature below 150°F. Most ovens don't go that low (my lowest setting is 200°F), so keep the oven door slightly ajar and use an oven thermometer to regulate the temperature. It's said that if you heat the nuts above 150°F, you'll destroy the good enzymes. If you're really dedicated to soaking, consider purchasing a food dehydrator.

If this all seems like a lot of hassle, you can dry your nuts in an oven set to 300 to 350°F with the same taste result—or you can just blend them into a butter without soaking at all. Unless you're a strict vegetarian or your diet is restricted in other ways, you're likely to get the nutrients you need from other foods and still reap the other positive benefits of nuts and seeds without soaking them.

Tools

SPATULA

A good strong, dishwasher-safe silicone spatula with some bend and flexibility may be the single most important tool you'll want when working with the blender. It will help scrape all the good bits out, and will also help push ingredients toward the blade. I have several different sizes, including a small one for scraping under the blade.

SHARP PARING KNIFE AND CHEF'S KNIFE

While the blender blades will do most of your cutting and chopping, it's still good to have sharp knives on hand to cut up large fruits like watermelon and do more tedious jobs like removing ribs from kale. Always hand wash your knives and dry them immediately after each use.

FINE-MESH STRAINER/SIEVE
You'll find this simple kitchen tool indispensable for juices and straining purees and sauces.

NUT BAGS
Although you can use cheesecloth or a sieve, I find that a sturdy nylon drawstring bag works best when straining nut and seed milks.

ICE CUBE TRAYS
Pour leftover smoothies and purees into ice cube trays to make frozen cubes, which are easy to store and blend up again quite well.

RESEALABLE FREEZER BAGS
Good to have on hand for freezing fruit and other blender leftovers.

STORAGE CONTAINERS
French-made Luminarc glasses with airtight plastic storage lids are perfect for storing soups, juices, and more. They fit well in the fridge, and I like that they double as drinking glasses.

METAL STRAWS
Many years ago, I had a colleague who looked at me disapprovingly every time I used a plastic straw. "Do you know how unnecessary that is?" she would say to me. And she was right. I don't think I saw one straw when I was traveling in France recently. The French seem to consume their beverages just fine without them.

According to ecocycle.org, we use over 500 million straws in the United States each day. There are a plethora of reasons why we shouldn't use disposable plastic straws, including growing landfills, so I try to use metal and biodegradable paper ones whenever possible.

CAST-IRON PAN
This may seem like an odd essential for blender cooking, but a well-seasoned cast-iron skillet will fry up a blender burger with a restaurant-quality crispy crust. Its nonstick surface is also great for pancakes, and you can even bake brownies in it. They're inexpensive and can take the place of four pans. If I were stuck on a desert island and could have one kitchen tool, this would be it (unless, of course, I could get a solar-powered blender!).

CHAPTER TWO

SMOOTHIES & HEALTHY DRINKS

Almond Milk

An excellent alternative to dairy milk, silky-smooth almond milk is low in carbs, cholesterol- and lactose-free, easy to digest, and a good source of vitamin E.

Makes about 3 cups

1 cup almonds, soaked for 8 hours, then drained with water discarded

3 cups spring water or filtered tap water

Sweetener to taste, if desired

Place the nuts and water in the blender jar and process on high until combined and completely smooth. Add sweetener if desired. Strain the mixture using a nut bag or strainer. Discard the pulp. Chill and serve.

Brown Rice Milk

For those with a lactose or nut intolerance, brown rice milk is a good cow's or nut milk substitute because it's unlikely to trigger allergic reactions. Rice milk, which has a light, refreshing flavor, is low in fat but high in carbs.

Makes about 3⅔ cups

¾ cup cooked brown rice

3 cups spring water or filtered tap water

Pinch of kosher salt

¼ teaspoon pure vanilla extract

Honey to taste, if desired

Place all the ingredients in the blender jar and process on high until combined and completely smooth. Discard the pulp. Strain the mixture using a nut bag or strainer. Chill and serve.

Coconut Milk

Rich with its creamy goodness and slight hint of coconut, this milk makes a delicious base for smoothies. Use it in cupcakes and muffins too.

Makes about 4½ cups

2 cups unsweetened coconut or coconut flakes

4 cups spring water or filtered tap water

Soak the coconut in the water for 2 hours. Place the coconut and the water in the blender jar and process on high for 2 minutes or until smooth. Strain the coconut through a nut bag, squeezing out all the milk into a bowl. When you've squeezed out all you can, transfer the milk to a storage container and reserve the pulp for another use. Chill and serve.

Hemp Seed Milk

Considered a superfood, hemp seeds are one of the densest sources of plant proteins available. These power-packed kernels deliver protein and omega-3 essential fatty acids, which are essential to brain, skin, joint, and heart health. You can sprinkle them raw on almost anything, and when you blend the seeds into a milk, they give the beverage an especially creamy consistency.

Makes about 4 cups

1 cup shelled organic hemp seeds (also called hemp hearts)

3 cups spring water or filtered tap water

1 teaspoon raw honey

Place all the ingredients in the blender jar and process on high until combined and completely smooth. Strain the mixture using a nut bag or strainer. Discard the pulp. Chill and serve.

Pure Strawberry-Banana Smoothie

Strawberries and bananas are enhanced by the sweet, earthy flavor of hemp milk, an extremely beneficial non-dairy milk alternative that is a breeze to make (page 26). It's hard to believe this creamy, dessert-like drink, with 10 essential amino acids, is actually good for you!

Serves 2

2 cups hemp milk (page 26)

2 frozen bananas, peeled and cut into large chunks

1 pint (2 cups) frozen strawberries, hulled

Place all the ingredients in the blender pitcher in the order listed above. Blend for 20 seconds on low, then turn to high for another 40 to 60 seconds or until the mixture is completely smooth.

Coconut-Almond Smoothie

Smooth and creamy, this milky drink has a pleasing nutty flavor. It's kind of like an Almond Joy without the chocolate. If you want it to mimic the candy bar even more, shave a little dark chocolate on top.

Serves 1

1 cup coconut milk (page 25)

1 tablespoon almond butter (page 54)

5 dates, pitted

1 teaspoon pure vanilla extract (optional)

1½ cups ice

Place all the ingredients in the blender pitcher in the order listed. Blend for 20 seconds on low, then turn to high for another 40 to 60 seconds or until the mixture is completely smooth.

Pumpkin-Spice Smoothie

Like the smell of burning leaves or apple cider doughnuts, this smoothie will transport you to a place of autumnal happiness any time of the year. Sip this creamy concoction through a straw and you'll swear you're slurping up a pumpkin pie.

Serves 2

1 cup canned pumpkin

1 cup coconut milk (page 25)

1 cup ice

1 small frozen banana, cut into several pieces

1 tablespoon maple syrup

½ teaspoon ground cinnamon

¼ teaspoon ground nutmeg

¼ teaspoon ground ginger

⅛ teaspoon ground cloves

¼ teaspoon orange zest

Place all the ingredients in the blender pitcher in the order listed. Blend for 5 seconds on low, then turn to high for another 20 seconds or until the mixture is completely smooth.

Revitalizing Raw Green Juice

Go green! A mix of fruits and veggies gives this drink an agreeable balance between sweet and bitter. Don't hesitate to mix up your greens here—kale, spinach, beet greens—for a variety of tastes. You can drink this as a smoothie, too; just skip the straining and add 1 cup ice when blending.

Serves 2

1 cup unsweetened iced green tea

½ apple, peeled, cored, and cut into quarters

2 Swiss chard leaves, stem removed

1 romaine leaf

¼ cucumber, seeded and cut into quarters

1 tablespoon freshly squeezed lemon juice

¼ cup flat-leaf parsley leaves

1-inch piece gingerroot, peeled

15 green grapes

Place all the ingredients in the blender pitcher in the order listed above. Blend for 10 seconds on medium, then turn to high for 1 more minute. Push the mixture through a fine-mesh strainer. Chill to serve or pour over ice.

Beet & Carrot Juice Tonic

Boost your stamina and immunity with this vitamin-loaded juice. The combination of carrots and beets does tend to become thick, though, so don't hesitate adding more water to obtain a thinner consistency. Pouring it over a full glass of ice will also help dilute this juice.

Serves 1

¼–½ cup coconut water or spring water, depending on desired consistency

1 medium orange, peeled and divided into sections

2 medium carrots, washed and cut into 2-inch chunks

3 beets (about 5–7 ounces total), washed and quartered

Place everything in the blender pitcher in the order listed. Blend on low for 30 seconds, turn the dial to medium and blend for 15 seconds more, then turn to high and blend for 1 minute. Push the mixture through a fine-mesh strainer. Blend a second time for an even smoother consistency. Chill to serve or pour over ice.

Cranberry-Orange Frappe

Fresh. Bright. Zingy. This vitamin C booster will wake up your taste buds with its citrusy tang. Not just for breakfast, this drink makes a stimulating afternoon snack.

Serves 2

½ cup almond milk (page 22)

1 cup frozen cranberries

1 whole orange, peeled and broken into segments

¼ teaspoon ground cinnamon

1–2 teaspoons maple syrup, or more to taste

1 cup ice

Place all the ingredients in the blender pitcher in the order listed. Blend for 20 seconds on low, then turn to high for another 40 to 60 seconds or until the mixture is completely smooth.

Refreshing Pineapple-Ginger Juice

I learned to make this downright addictive drink from a bartender at The Rockhouse in Negril, Jamaica. After seeing it listed on the breakfast menu under juices simply as "Homemade," my family and I were intrigued. One morning we took the plunge and ordered it. We never looked back. When I asked the waitress about the fresh and spicy drink, she told me the bartenders made it. The very friendly Naason showed me how. He blended up the whole pineapple, peel and all, in his Vitamix. It takes a little time, but it is worth every second of effort. It's also inviting as an afternoon cocktail with a little Jamaican rum.

Serves 4

1 whole pineapple, cored and cut into chunks

⅓ cup (2 ounces) fresh peeled gingerroot, chopped

2 cups spring water or filtered tap water

Raw honey to taste

Place the pineapple, ginger, and water in a blender and process on medium-high until the mixture is fully blended (as smooth as you can get it). Place a fine-mesh strainer over a bowl or container and pour in the pineapple-ginger mixture. Using the back of a spoon, press the mixture against the strainer, extracting as much of the juice as possible. You could use a nut bag, too. Put the pineapple mash in the strainer back into the blender and process again on high. Strain again to extract more liquid from the mixture. After your second strain, you should have about 36 ounces. If not, you may want to blend and strain the mixture one more time. Finally, add honey to taste and stir to combine. Chill and serve over ice. Cool

Cool Mint Slush

Refreshing and smooth, this icy concoction will cool you down on the hottest of days. A splash of vodka or gin turns this drink into a delightful summer cocktail. Whip up a batch in advance and freeze in a resealable plastic bag. When you're ready to use it, break up the mixture in the sealed bag then add it to the blender container, pulse several times, and serve.

Serves 4–6

1 whole lemon, cut into quarters, seeds removed

¾ cup freshly squeezed lemon juice (juice of about 3 lemons)

⅓ cup raw honey, or more to taste

¼ cup water

4 cups ice

½ cup fresh mint leaves, plus extra for garnish

Add the cut lemon and lemon juice to the container and blend on medium-high until smooth. Add the honey, water, and ice and continue to blend until completely smooth. Put the mint in the container and pulse five or six times, until the mint is chopped and mixed throughout. Serve garnished with mint leaves.

Mango & Greek Yogurt Freeze

This drink delivers the essence of mangoes, which are at their best in spring and summer. Mangoes that are green and hard should ripen after a few days at room temperature. The feel and smell of the mango are much more important than the color. Never refrigerate unripe mangoes. If ripe mangoes aren't available, look for jarred mango in the produce section or bags of mango chunks in the frozen food section. When mangoes are in season (and usually on sale), I buy them in bulk, cut the fruit into chunks, and freeze it in airtight containers.

Serves 1

1 cup fresh mango chunks

½ cup plain Greek yogurt

1 cup ice

1 teaspoon raw honey or other sweetener to taste

Place all the ingredients in the blender pitcher in the order listed. Blend for 20 seconds on low then turn to high for another 40 to 60 seconds or until the mixture is completely smooth.

Watermelon-Cucumber *Agua Fresca*

Agua fresca or "fresh water" is simply water infused with the essence of fruit. The thirst-quenching drink has just a hint of flavor. It's not too sweet, and is best when made with seasonally fresh fruit (experiment with different combinations including melons, pineapple, and mango). Serve it icy cold.

Makes 2 quarts

4 cups spring water or filtered tap water

½ large watermelon, cut into large chunks (about 8 generous cups)

1 cucumber (about 2 cups)

¼ cup raw honey or to taste

6 basil leaves, for garnish

Put half the water, watermelon, and cucumber in the blender and run on low for 5 seconds. Then turn to high and process for 25 seconds or until pureed. Push the mixture through a fine-mesh strainer into a 2-quart pitcher. Repeat the process with the rest of the ingredients, adding the honey this time. Pour the second strained mixture into the first. Stir and chill. Serve over ice and garnish with basil leaves.

CHAPTER THREE

BREAKFASTS

Buckwheat Waffles with Two-Berry Coulis

Do you know that buckwheat has nothing to do with wheat? It's not even a grain. It's a flowering herb whose starchy seeds are harvested and are available in many forms, from hulled, whole raw kernels to ground flours. In this recipe I use light buckwheat flour because it gives a lighter texture to the waffles. I am partial to Bouchard Family Farms Acadian Light Buckwheat Flour. If you can't find it and use dark buckwheat flour (which is visibly darker in appearance), use 1 cup white whole wheat flour in place of 1 cup buckwheat flour for these waffles. Buckwheat flour makes a great fried chicken coating too. Fried chicken and waffles anyone?

Makes about fifteen 7-inch waffles

3 large eggs

2 cups buttermilk

1 teaspoon pure vanilla extract

1¾ cups light buckwheat flour

¼ cup organic cane sugar

¼ teaspoon kosher salt

1 tablespoon baking powder

½ cup aroma-free coconut oil, melted, or canola oil

Fresh blackberries, red raspberries, and strawberries

Two-Berry Coulis (recipe follows)

Put the eggs, buttermilk, and vanilla in the blender. Process on medium for 15 seconds. Next, add the flour, sugar, salt, and baking powder. Pulse several more times until the ingredients are just combined. Lastly, add the oil and pulse until mixed together. Bake in a preheated waffle iron on a medium setting. Make sure the waffles bake until they're somewhat crispy. Serve with fresh berries and Two-Berry Coulis.

TWO-BERRY COULIS

1 pint (2 cups) red raspberries

1 pint (2 cups) strawberries

¼ cup water

3 tablespoons organic cane sugar, or to taste, depending on the sweetness of the berries

Put the berries, water, and sugar in a small saucepan. Cook over medium heat, stirring constantly, for about 10 minutes. Next, pour the mixture in the blender and run for 10 seconds on high. Pour the mixture through a fine-mesh strainer back into the saucepan. Use the back of a spoon to push as much of the sauce through the sieve as possible and bring it to a gentle boil for 3 minutes. Allow to cool. Serve over Buckwheat Waffles.

Sweet Spelt Flour Crêpes

This recipe belongs to my 13-year-old daughter, who has been making crêpes since she was 9. A self-taught crêpe maker, Camilla got a few pointers from a good friend of ours who lives in Montréal, and another book tipped her off to the magic of the blender—using it whips up crêpe batter to the perfect consistency.

When in France recently we noticed that many savory crêpes were made with buckwheat, which led us to experiment with different flours. I've made my own adjustment to Camilla's recipe and substituted spelt flour for the white flour she uses. It gives a faint nutty flavor to the thin pancakes, which are so delectable they barely need a filling. A squeeze of lemon and sprinkle of sugar is the perfect comple-ment to the delicate pancake, although a few strawberries and hazelnut spread are pretty darn good on them, too.

Makes about 14 crêpes

4 large eggs

2 cups milk

½ teaspoon pure vanilla extract

2 cups spelt flour

½ teaspoon kosher salt

¼ cup melted unsalted butter, plus more for greasing the pan

Put the eggs, milk, and vanilla in the blender and process on medium for 15 seconds. Add the flour and salt and pulse several times. Add the butter and mix for 10 more seconds. Melt about 2 teaspoons butter over medium heat in a nonstick 12-inch skillet. Spread the butter evenly around. Pour 2 to 3 table-spoons of batter in the pan. Cook for 1 minute then flip the crêpe over and cook for another minute. The thinner the batter, the better. Continue to cook crêpes until all the batter is used.

Chia Seed Pancakes

Chia seeds, which can be eaten whole, don't need to be ground to access their great health benefits. Tiny black and white chia seeds are a great source of protein and calcium and will boost the fiber content of your pancakes while giving them the slightest crunchy texture. Sounds strange for a pancake, I know, but it really adds an interesting new dimension to an old favorite.

Makes about twenty 4-inch pancakes

2 cups buttermilk

1 large egg

1 teaspoon pure vanilla extract

1 tablespoon organic cane sugar

1½ cups white whole wheat flour

1 tablespoon baking powder

2 tablespoons chia seeds

1–2 tablespoons coconut oil or unsalted butter

Put the buttermilk, egg, and vanilla in the blender pitcher. Pulse on medium several times. Next, add the sugar, flour, and baking powder to the pitcher and pulse again two or three times until just blended. Do not overmix; this will result in tough pancakes. Add the chia seeds and pulse one more time. Place a griddle or frying pan over medium heat. Add 1 tablespoon of the coconut oil or butter and use a spatula to spread it around the griddle or pan as it melts.

Transfer the batter from the blender pitcher to the griddle or skillet using a tablespoon measure, about 2 tablespoons per pancake. Spread the batter into a circle shape with the back of the spoon. Cook until small bubbles appear and start to burst uniformly over the pancakes. Carefully flip the pancakes and cook for several more minutes on the other side. When golden brown on both sides, transfer to a serving platter. Continue to cook pancakes until all the batter is used, adding more oil or butter to the pan as needed. Serve with warm maple syrup.

Two-Bite Raspberry Financiers

These little French-inspired cakes get their distinct flavor from beurre noisette or brown butter. They are the perfect early-morning snack to serve to awaiting guests.

Makes 24

½ cup (1 stick) unsalted butter, cut into 1-inch pieces, plus more for greasing the pans

¾ cup almond flour

¼ cup all-purpose flour

⅔ cup confectioners' sugar

½ teaspoon baking powder

⅛ teaspoon kosher salt

5 large egg whites

1 teaspoon raw honey

½ teaspoon vanilla extract

½ pint (1 cup) red raspberries

Heat the butter in a small pan over medium-high heat, stirring it constantly. Keep stirring as the butter begins to bubble and foam. It will begin to brown in about 3 to 4 minutes (you'll see small bits on the bottom of the pan). When it does, remove it from the heat and set aside. Note that the butter goes from brown to burned very quickly. Put the flours, sugar, baking powder, and salt in the blender and run for 10 seconds on high. Using a spatula, scrape the flours from the bottom of the mixer and run for another 10 seconds. Add the egg whites, honey, and vanilla; pulse three times. Do not overmix. Transfer the batter to a bowl and stir in the browned butter. Cover with plastic wrap and refrigerate for at least 2 hours or up to 5 days. Heat the oven to 400°F. Thoroughly butter a 24-cup mini muffin pan. Remove the batter from the refrigerator and stir. Fill each cup with a tablespoon of batter and top with one or two red raspberries. Bake for 13 to 15 minutes or until the financiers are lightly browned and they spring back when touched."

Smooth Almond Butter

My go-to breakfast: a piece of whole grain toast topped with creamy almond butter and a sliced apple. This nut butter is high in iron, magnesium, and fiber, plus it offers a good dose of vitamin E.

Makes 1¾ cups

3 cups raw almonds

2 tablespoons coconut oil, melted,
plus more for rubbing the sides

Soak the almonds for 8 hours or overnight. Drain and rinse the nuts, then spread them on a parchment-lined baking sheet in a single layer. Bake them in the oven for 1½ hours at 300°F or until they are completely dry. Rub the inside of the blender jar with melted coconut oil. Place the nuts in the blender with the oil and run on low for 10 seconds. Then turn the blender to high and run for approximately 2 more minutes until the nuts become smooth and creamy.

Rich Coconut Butter

Spread this tasty tropical treat on toast in place of cow's butter, or use a spoonful in smoothies or sauces. One tablespoon contains two grams of fiber!

Makes 1 cup

4 cups unsweetened coconut flakes
(12-ounce package such as Bob's Red Mill)

Place the coconut flakes in the blender and run for 30 seconds on medium speed. Using a spatula, scrape down the sides and bottom of the blender jar, pushing the coconut toward the blade. Run the blender on high for 2½ minutes or until the mixture becomes smooth and creamy. Store in a jar at room temperature for up to three months (if you don't eat it sooner!).

CHAPTER FOUR

SOUPS & DIPS

Fresh Pineapple-Mango Salsa

This salsa sings summer. It reminds me of eating dinner outside on the patio with candles flickering just after sunset. On the menu: Grilled fish tacos. A warm corn tortilla stuffed with grilled tilapia, shredded cabbage, a scoop of guac, and a nice big spoonful of Pineapple Mango Salsa. It makes my mouth water just thinking about it.

Makes 2 cups

1-inch piece gingerroot, peeled

½ jalapeño, seeded and cut in half

2 tablespoons freshly squeezed lime juice

1 ripe mango, peeled and cut into large chunks (about 1 cup)

½ pineapple, peeled and cut into chunks (2 heaping cups)

¼ cup fresh mint leaves

Put the ginger, jalapeño, and lime juice in the blender and run for 10 seconds on medium. Using a spatula, push the ingredients toward the blade. Add the mango, pineapple, and mint to the blender and pulse three or four more times. The salsa should be somewhat chunky.

Simply Guac

My husband is an ever-so-diligent guacamole maker. He grinds the garlic and salt into a paste, finely chops the onion and cilantro, and carefully smashes the avocados by hand. The result is outstanding but the method definitely takes effort.

Without sounding like an infomercial, you can achieve something pretty comparable in mere minutes. Yup, you know it. The blender. Pulse ever-so-gingerly and you've got it, Simply Guac.

Makes about 2 cups

1 garlic clove, peeled

¼ cup fresh cilantro leaves

¼ small red onion, cut into chunks (about ¼ cup)

½ jalapeño, or more to taste, seeded and cut in half (about 2 teaspoons)

2 tablespoons freshly squeezed lime juice

½ teaspoon kosher salt

½ small tomato, cut in half and seeded

3 avocados, peeled, pitted, and cut in half

Put the garlic, cilantro, onion, jalapeño, lime juice, and salt in the blender and pulse two or three times. Add the tomato and the avocado and pulse two more times. Garnish with a few cilantro leaves before serving.

Super-Easy Edamame Dip

Be sure to save a few edamame to garnish this scrumptious green dip that can easily be mistaken for guacamole. Even with the telltale beans on top, you're still likely to get a few quizzical looks. I can almost guarantee one guest will ask, "Just what exactly is in this dip?"

Makes about 2 cups

3 trimmed scallions, white parts only

1 garlic clove, peeled

2 cups shelled edamame, cooked

½ cup water

1 tablespoon freshly squeezed lime juice

2 tablespoons sesame oil

1 tablespoon white miso paste

1 teaspoon soy sauce

½ cup fresh cilantro leaves

½ teaspoon sriracha, if desired

Put the scallions and garlic clove in the blender container and pulse several times. Using a spatula, scrape the garlic and scallions down from the sides of the pitcher. Add the rest of the ingredients listed above and process until smooth. Add salt to taste.

Smoky Hummus with Artichokes

Paper or plastic? Canned or dried? Is there a right answer? I can't really say. I do know that they all have their advantages. The biggest one to canned beans is the fast factor. You can decide you want hummus one minute and the next it's in front of you, ready to be devoured.

Dried beans take more planning, but I do think their taste and texture are superior. There are numerous other benefits to dried beans (more cost-effective, less packaging, et cetera), but don't let those keep you from eating canned beans, which have all the nutritional value of dried.

As for paper or plastic? I guess I'll just avoid the question and take my own bags.

Makes about 4 cups

1 small garlic clove, peeled

1 cup dried chickpeas, cooked and peeled, or 2 (15-ounce) cans beans, rinsed and drained

½ cup cooking water or liquid from the canned chickpeas

¼ teaspoon cayenne pepper

1 teaspoon smoked paprika

⅓ cup tahini

1½ tablespoons freshly squeezed lemon juice

¼ cup extra-virgin olive oil

1 teaspoon kosher salt

1 (14-ounce) can artichoke hearts, drained

Put the garlic in the blender and pulse one or two times. Add the rest of the ingredients except for the artichokes and process on medium speed for 30 seconds. Add the artichokes and pulse three or four more times. Do not overprocess; you want some artichoke pieces to remain for texture.

Mushroom Pâté

Woodsy and earthy, this tasty terrine makes an impressive vegetarian appetizer. Spread it on a warm, crusty piece of baguette and you'll leave your guests swooning. If you have leftover pâté, heat it up in a skillet with a little cream and chicken broth for a quick yet exquisite pasta sauce.

Makes about 3 cups

2 tablespoons extra-virgin olive oil, plus extra for oiling the ramekin

3 small shallots, peeled and sliced

2 garlic cloves, peeled and sliced

1½ pounds mixed fresh mushrooms, such as portobello, crimini, shiitake, and oyster

¼ cup flat-leaf parsley leaves

1 tablespoon fresh thyme

½ teaspoon kosher salt

⅛ teaspoon freshly ground black pepper

1 cup cashews, soaked for 2 hours and drained

½ teaspoon freshly squeezed lemon juice

Heat the oil in a skillet over medium heat and add the shallots, sautéing them for 5 minutes. Then add the garlic, mushrooms, parsley, thyme, salt, and pepper, and sauté for another 5 minutes. Transfer the mushroom mixture to the blender and add the cashews and lemon juice. Pulse several times until the mixture is combined but some texture still remains. Spoon into a well-oiled ramekin and cover tightly with plastic wrap. Chill for at least 2 hours or overnight. Serve on warm baguette rounds.

Autumn Squash & Pear Soup

Slightly sweet from the addition of pear, this beautiful golden soup says autumn like no other. You'll get a good healthy dose of beta-carotene and vitamin C from a bowlful, as well as a very happy belly.

Serves 6

3 acorn or 2 buttercup squash (or any assorted fall squash), about 4 pounds total, cut in half or quarters and seeded

2 tablespoons extra-virgin olive oil, divided

3 carrots, peeled and cut into 2-inch chunks

1 medium onion, sliced

4 cups (32 ounces) chicken broth, divided

2 pears, any variety, peeled and cored, cut into quarters

1 teaspoon kosher salt

¼ teaspoon freshly ground pepper

¼ teaspoon ground cinnamon

Maple syrup for serving

Preheat the oven to 375°F. Place the squash cut-side up on a baking sheet lined with parchment paper and drizzle with 1 tablespoon of the oil. Bake for 1 hour. Meanwhile, heat the second tablespoon of olive oil in a Dutch oven over medium-high heat. Add the carrots and onion and sauté for about 8 minutes or until the onion is softened. Set aside. When the squash is fully cooked and cooled enough to handle, scoop it out of the skin and put half of it in the blender. Add 2 cups of the broth, pears, carrots, onion, salt, pepper, and cinnamon, in that order. Start the blender on low and process for 10 seconds, turning it to high and processing until velvety smooth. Return the blended soup to the Dutch oven. Next process the remaining squash and broth until smooth and add that to the pot as well. Warm the puréed soup on the stove top until heated through. Serve with a drizzle of maple syrup.

Hearty Kale & Potato Soup

I apologize if you're tired of hearing me say blend lightly, but I have to underscore the importance of it once more with this recipe. Potatoes can easily turn to glue in the blender. When blended with diligence, this soup is thick and rewarding. The addition of kale after blending gives a delightful toothsome texture to the soup.

Serves 6–8

2 tablespoons extra-virgin olive oil

1 onion (about 1¼ cups), coarsely chopped

1 garlic clove, sliced

3 large baking potatoes (about 2¼ pounds total), peeled and cut into large chunks

7 cups chicken broth, divided

3–4 cups kale (about 4 large leaves), stems removed and coarsely chopped

¾ pound cooked kielbasa sausage, cut into ¾-inch-thick rounds

½ teaspoon freshly ground black pepper

1½ teaspoons kosher salt

Heat the olive oil in a Dutch oven over medium-high heat. Add the onion and garlic and sauté 5 to 8 minutes or until softened. Add the potatoes and sauté another 3 minutes, stirring frequently. Pour in 6 cups of the broth and bring to a boil. Reduce the heat and simmer for 15 minutes. When the potatoes are cooked through, pour the soup in the blender and pulse three or four times on high or until almost smooth, in two batches if necessary. Do not process for more than 30 seconds as the soup will become gummy. Pour the soup back in the Dutch oven, adding the kale, sausage, and remaining 1 cup broth, pepper, and salt. Simmer for another 10 minutes, until the kale has softened and the sausage is heated through.

Spicy Chickpea Soup

Rich with the flavor of chickpeas, this homey, satiating soup includes fire-roasted tomatoes and paprika for a vibrant spice. It's the kind of soup you want to dip a thick, gooey grilled cheese into.

Serves 6

3 tablespoons extra-virgin olive oil

2 garlic cloves, finely diced

1 large onion, peeled and cut into medium dice

2 teaspoons smoked paprika

1 teaspoon ground cumin

½ teaspoon turmeric

½ teaspoon kosher salt

1 (28-ounce) can diced fire-roasted tomatoes, such as Muir Glen

2 (15-ounce) cans chickpeas, rinsed and drained

4 cups chicken broth

Salt and freshly ground pepper to taste

¼ cup flat-leaf parsley, finely chopped, for garnish

Lemon zest, for garnish

Heat the oil over medium heat in a large soup pot or Dutch oven. Sauté the garlic and onion for 8 to 10 minutes or until softened. Add the spices and seasonings and sauté for another 2 minutes. Add the tomatoes, chickpeas, and broth. Simmer for 5 minutes. Using a ladle, spoon half the soup into the blender jar and process for 45 seconds on medium. Pour the pureed soup back into the pot and stir together. Add salt and pepper to taste. Heat through and serve with chopped parsley and lemon zest for garnish.

Green Gazpacho

While many think of gazpacho as a spicy tomato-based soup, there are many variations to be found in Spain, its origin country, and this is one of them. Inspired by summer's bountiful harvest, this tomato-less soup combines a plethora of healthy green veggies. Serve it cold in shot glasses or in a small mug for a cheerful presentation.

Serves 6

2 cucumbers, seeded and cut into large chunks (about 3 cups)

1 small zucchini, cut into large chunks (about 1 heaping cup)

1 cup shelled peas, blanched

½ small yellow onion, coarsely chopped (about ¾ cup)

1 green bell pepper, seeds removed, cut into quarters

3 tablespoons freshly squeezed lemon juice

¼ cup extra-virgin olive oil

2 tablespoons white wine vinegar

1 teaspoon organic cane sugar

1 teaspoon kosher salt

1 garlic clove

¼ teaspoon ground coriander

1 teaspoon ground cumin

Pinch of freshly ground white pepper

1–2 cups spring water or filtered tap water

Plain Greek yogurt and freshly cut chives, for garnish

Place all the ingredients (except the yogurt and chives) in the blender in the order listed. Process on low for 20 seconds, then turn to high and run on high until velvety smooth. Chill for at least 2 hours and serve with a small dollop of plain Greek yogurt and freshly cut chives.

CHAPTER FIVE

SALADS & VEGETABLES

Chopped Kale Salad

This salad is substantial, as are the parts that make it. Not all salad leaves can withstand the power of the blender, but kale can. Remove the ribs, add the leaves to your blender jar with water, and your blades will do all the work. You'll need to repeat this action several times for each vegetable added to the salad—they take different times to dice up, and you'll need to drain each element thoroughly—but it's worth it. The result is a crunchy, uniformly chopped salad.

Serves 4-6

FOR THE SALAD

¾ cup pine nuts

1 bunch kale, ribs and stems removed

2 carrots, peeled and cut into 2-inch chunks

6 radishes, cut in half

2 ounces blue cheese, crumbled (about 3 heaping tablespoons)

FOR THE DRESSING

1 garlic clove, peeled

½ avocado, pitted and peeled

¼ cup freshly squeezed lemon juice (juice of about 2 lemons)

1 tablespoon Dijon mustard

2 tablespoons water

1 tablespoon raw honey

½ cup extra-virgin olive oil

Put the pine nuts in a skillet and toast for about 5 minutes over medium heat, stirring constantly. Set aside to cool. Next, put the kale in the blender and add

4 cups of water. Pulse 8 to 10 times with short, quick pulses. Drain the greens and put them in a large salad bowl lined with paper towels. Add the carrots and radishes to the blender and fill with enough water to cover the vegetables. Pulse several times until chopped, drain, and add to the salad bowl. To make the dressing: Place the garlic in the blender jar and pulse several times. Add the rest of the ingredients, except the olive oil. Process on high for 30 seconds. Add the oil and continue to blend until thoroughly mixed. Remove the paper towels from the bottom of the bowl and toss the salad with the dressing and pine nuts. Sprinkle with the blue cheese. Toss a few more times and serve.

Asian Slaw

The texture of shredded coleslaw is a nice complement to many main courses, especially grilled fish and chicken. For a more traditional slaw, mix shredded cabbage with aioli. This recipe uses a water chopping method that quickly dices large amounts of vegetables. However, it is very important that you drain the vegetables completely or you'll end up with a watery mess. Use extra paper towels if necessary to absorb the excess water.

Serves 4-6

½ head cabbage, cored and cut into quarters

2 carrots, peeled and cut into 2-inch chunks

1 whole scallion, trimmed and cut into 2-inch chunks

1 tablespoon soy sauce

1 tablespoon lime juice

1 tablespoon sesame oil

2 tablespoons rice wine vinegar

2 teaspoons dark brown sugar

½-inch piece fresh gingerroot, peeled

1 garlic clove, peeled

1 tablespoon water

Put the cabbage in the blender and cover with water. Pulse four or five times or until finely chopped. Drain in a fine-mesh sieve and put into a paper-towel-lined bowl. Place a doubled paper towel on top of the cabbage. Repeat the blender-water chopping with the carrots and scallion at the same time. Drain the mixture in the sieve and put it on top of the paper towel. Put all the remaining ingredients in the cleaned blender jar and process on high until smooth. Remove the paper towel from the bowl and toss the slaw with the dressing. Refrigerate until you're ready to serve.

Carrot Quinoa Salad

Quinoa is a quick and easy way to add protein to a salad. It's also gluten-free and deeply gratifying. This salad holds well and makes a great lunch-on-the-go.

Serves 4

FOR THE SALAD

1 cup quinoa

2 cups diced carrots (about 1 pound)

2 teaspoons extra-virgin olive oil

¼ teaspoon kosher salt

FOR THE DRESSING

1 tablespoon tahini

1 tablespoon soy sauce

1 tablespoon freshly squeezed lemon juice

1 tablespoon sesame oil

¼ teaspoon sriracha

1 tablespoon water

1 bunch scallions (about 5), trimmed and cut into 2-inch pieces

Rinse and cook the quinoa according to the package's instructions. Meanwhile, preheat the oven to 400°F. Place the diced carrots on a baking sheet and toss with the olive oil and salt. Roast the carrots for 15 minutes, tossing twice during that time. To make the dressing, place all the ingredients minus one scallion in the blender pitcher and process for 1 minute on high. Toss the cooked quinoa and carrots with the dressing and chop the remaining scallion for garnish.

French Lentil Salad with Roasted Tomato Vinaigrette

Slow-roasted tomatoes are sweet and addictive. You may want to double the amount you roast so you can have extras to snack on. The fragrant smell of the roasting onions and tomatoes always gets my kids in the kitchen asking, "What are you cooking, Mom?" They usually stay pretty close by until the salad is tossed up.

Serves 4

FOR THE SALAD

1 pint cherry tomatoes, cut in half

½ large red onion, sliced (about 1½ cups)

1 tablespoon extra-virgin olive oil

1 tablespoon balsamic vinegar

1 teaspoon organic cane sugar

1 cup green lentils, rinsed

1 bay leaf

1 garlic clove, peeled

1 carrot, washed and cut into 2-inch chunks

3 cups arugula

½ cup crumbled feta cheese

FOR THE VINAIGRETTE

3 tablespoons extra-virgin olive oil

2 tablespoons balsamic vinegar

¾ teaspoon kosher salt

Preheat the oven to 350°F. Line a baking sheet with parchment paper. Place the tomatoes and onion in a bowl and toss with the oil, balsamic, and sugar. Spread them evenly on the pan, flat-side down, and bake for 25 minutes. Meanwhile, put the lentils, bay leaf, garlic clove, and carrot in a saucepan and cover with 2 inches of water. Bring to a boil. Simmer over moderate heat about 30 minutes, or until the lentils are tender. To make the vinaigrette: While the lentils are cooking, place ¼ cup of the roasted tomatoes in the blender with the oil, vinegar, and salt. Blend on high for 30 seconds or until thoroughly combined. Drain any excess water from the lentils, remove the bay leaf, carrot, and garlic, and put in a bowl with the remaining ¾ cup of tomatoes, roasted onion, arugula, and feta. Toss with the vinaigrette and serve.

Go-To Herb Vinaigrette

How is it that the French can make simple salad greens taste so splendid? Every time? I find the majority of restaurants in France, from the north to south, serve a small handful of dressed greens with the sheerest vinaigrette that is consistently ever-so-tantalizing. What is it, then, that makes a French vinaigrette authentic? Perhaps it's the quality of the olive oil and Dijon, or the fresh, delicate herbs. We'll call this blend my "Ffrench" vinaigrette. It's my daily go-to salad dressing. Hopefully it'll beckon you to eat your greens like those blends in France do.

Makes about ½ cup

1 small shallot, peeled

2 tablespoons red wine vinegar

½ teaspoon kosher salt

¼ teaspoon freshly ground black pepper

¼ teaspoon organic cane sugar

1 teaspoon Dijon mustard

2 teaspoons fresh tarragon

2 teaspoons fresh thyme

1 teaspoon fresh oregano

⅓ cup extra-virgin olive oil

Put the shallot in the blender and run on high for 10 seconds. Scrape the shallot off the sides of the blender toward the blade using a spatula. Add the vinegar, salt, pepper, sugar, and mustard. Process again on medium for another 20 seconds. Add the herbs and process again for 10 seconds. Lastly, add the olive oil and run the blender for 1 minute on high or until the dressing is thoroughly combined and the herbs are finely chopped. Stop the blender and scrape down the sides as necessary. Serve over mesclun or other desired greens.

Bibb Lettuce with Grapefruit-Shallot Vinaigrette

The sweet and tart dressing here lightly coats the delicate Bibb leaves of this salad, which are balanced by the slight crunch of sunflower seed kernels.

Serves 4

2 shallots, peeled and sliced (about ¼ cup)

½ cup, plus 1 tablespoon extra-virgin olive oil, divided

⅓ cup, plus 1 tablespoon grapefruit juice, divided

1 teaspoon organic cane sugar

1 teaspoon Dijon mustard

1 tablespoon orange marmalade

1 teaspoon fresh rosemary

½ teaspoon kosher salt

¼ teaspoon freshly ground black pepper

1 head Bibb lettuce

1 grapefruit, peeled and cut into segments

½ cup ricotta salata (1 ounce), shaved with a vegetable peeler

¼ cup hulled sunflower seeds

In a small saucepan, sauté the shallots in 1 tablespoon of the olive oil for about 4 minutes. Sprinkle with 1 tablespoon of the grapefruit juice and sugar. Cook on low for 8 to 10 minutes. Whisk in the rest of the grapefruit juice and mustard to the shallot mixture and cook over medium-high heat until it comes to a gentle boil. Stir in the orange marmalade, rosemary, salt, and pepper; cook for another minute. Transfer the mixture to the blender, add the remaining ½ cup olive oil, and process for 1 minute or until smooth. Toss with the remaining ingredients and serve.

Creamy Cauliflower Mash

This low-carb alternative to mashed potatoes is so silky and smooth that you may find you like it better than traditional spuds, which can turn out lumpy, bumpy, and gluey. Just make sure you drain the cauliflower really well after boiling it, perhaps even placing it on a paper towel for a few minutes before pureeing to prevent a watery texture.

Serves 4

1 head cauliflower, cleaned, cored, and cut into florets

1 garlic clove, peeled

1 tablespoon cream cheese

2 tablespoons grated Parmesan cheese

3 tablespoons milk

½ teaspoon kosher salt

Freshly ground black pepper to taste

Bring a large pot of water to a boil. Add the cauliflower florets and garlic clove. Bring the water back to a boil then reduce the heat to medium-low and simmer for 8 minutes. After 8 minutes, check that the cauliflower is fork-tender. If not, continue to cook until it is. Drain well. Add the drained cauliflower, garlic clove, cheeses, milk, and salt to the blender pitcher. Run on medium for 30 seconds, using a spatula to scrape down the sides of the pitcher as necessary. Pour the mash into a serving bowl. Add black pepper to taste and stir well.

Herbed Carrot-Parsnip Purée

There's something very satisfying about this sweet and creamy dish, which makes it a year-round favorite. The bright orange puree is light enough to serve in summer, yet is also nourishing enough to be comforting in winter.

Serves 4

1½ pounds carrots (about 9 medium), peeled and cut into 2-inch chunks

¾ pound parsnips (about 3), peeled and cut into 2-inch chunks

1 garlic clove, peeled

¼ cup coconut milk

5 teaspoons extra-virgin olive oil

2 teaspoons fresh thyme

Place the carrots, parsnips, and garlic in a 2-quart pot filled three-quarters with water. Bring the water to a boil, then turn the heat down and simmer the carrots and parsnips for about 15 minutes or until the vegetables are fork-tender. When the vegetables are done cooking, drain them and put them in the blender container with the rest of the ingredients. Process for about 30 seconds on medium or until the mixture becomes creamy and smooth. Serve immediately.

Roasted Root Veggies with Romesco Sauce

Romesco is a garlicky sauce that originated in Spain. I've encountered quite a few variations on this mild sauce over the years, and seen it used in many ways—over vegetables, with fish, and even with a salad. Here I've paired it with roasted vegetables, but it's even good just spread on a piece of warm baguette.

Serves 6

1 ancho chile, cored and seeded

3 red peppers, seeded and cut in half lengthwise, or 1 (24-ounce) jar roasted peppers

⅓ cup hazelnuts, skinned

1 (14-ounce) can fire-roasted tomatoes, such as Muir Glen

3 garlic cloves, peeled

2 tablespoons flat-leaf parsley, plus extra for garnish

2 tablespoons red wine vinegar

1 teaspoon smoked paprika

¼ cup, plus 2 tablespoons extra-virgin olive oil, divided

3-pound assortment of root vegetables (such as carrots, parsnips, purple and white potatoes, and sweet potatoes), peeled and cut into 2-inch cubes

½ teaspoon kosher salt

¼ teaspoon freshly ground black pepper

Preheat the oven to 450°F. Place the ancho chile in a bowl and cover it with boiling water. Allow it to sit for 30 minutes, then drain. Place the red peppers on a foil-lined baking sheet and set in the oven for 40 minutes or until the skins have begun to char and are wrinkled. Then remove the peppers from the oven and immediately put them in a brown paper bag to steam. Make sure the top of the bag is tightly rolled down to create a seal.

After about 15 minutes, the peppers should be cool enough to handle and you will be able to easily remove the skins. Reduce the oven temperature to 400°F. Meanwhile, put the hazelnuts in the blender and pulse them until they're coarsely ground. When your peppers are ready, add them to the blender with the reserved chile, tomatoes, garlic, parsley, vinegar, paprika, and ¼ cup of the oil. Purée until smooth.

Put the cubed vegetables on a baking sheet and toss with the remaining 2 tablespoons olive oil and the salt and pepper. Roast for 40 minutes or until tender and golden, turning the vegetables several times with a spatula while roasting. Transfer the roasted vegetables to a bowl and toss with Romesco Sauce. Garnish with chopped parsley and serve.

CHAPTER SIX

MAIN DISHES

Family-Favorite Salmon Burgers with Quick-Pickled Cukes

These robust burgers will give beef burgers a run for their money any day—they are big, juicy, and flavorful just like a burger should be. Watercress adds a nice bite to the firm but not-too-firm texture. Since ketchup isn't an option here (or at least I hope not!), the Quick Pickled Cukes are a must. Their zesty crunch makes them the perfect condiment.

Serves 4

FOR THE BURGERS

1 pound skinless, boneless salmon fillet, cut into large chunks

3 ounces smoked salmon

1 large egg

¾ cup watercress

1 teaspoon lemon zest

⅛ teaspoon freshly ground black pepper

1 tablespoon extra-virgin olive oil

FOR THE QUICK-PICKLED CUKES

½ cup white vinegar

1 tablespoon organic cane sugar

¼ teaspoon crushed red pepper flakes

⅛ teaspoon kosher salt

1 whole cucumber, very thinly sliced

To make the cukes: Combine the vinegar, sugar, pepper flakes, and salt in a bowl; add the cucumber slices. Cover with plastic wrap and allow to marinate for at least 30 minutes before serving. To make the burgers, place all the ingredients (except the oil) in the blender and pulse four to five times until just combined. The mixture should be chunky. Form the mixture into four patties and place on waxed paper. Heat the oil in a skillet over medium-high heat. Carefully slide the patties into the heated skillet and cook for about 4 minutes on each side or until heated through. Serve on buns with Quick Pickled Cukes.

Super-Satisfying Beet & Chickpea Burgers

Don't let the list of ingredients here scare you. I know it seems long and perhaps daunting. With the help of the blender, though, everything gets mixed up in a snap. The balance of beans and vegetables and brown rice is important to achieving a vegetarian burger that's more than just mush. Dipping the burger in bread crumbs before frying gives a crispy golden crust to the patty.

Serves 4-6

4 tablespoons extra-virgin olive oil, divided

2 tablespoons balsamic vinegar

2 garlic cloves, peeled and cut in half

1 (6-ounce) beet, peeled and cut into chunks

3 carrots (about 1 generous cup), peeled and cut into 2-inch chunks

1 large red onion (about 2 cups), cut into large chunks

½ cup cooked brown rice

⅓ cup oat flour

1 large egg

1 teaspoon ground cumin

½ teaspoon ground coriander

3 cups cooked chickpeas or 2 (15-ounce) cans chickpeas, drained and rinsed

⅓ cup finely ground whole wheat bread crumbs

Goat cheese and mixed baby sprouts (available from farmers' markets), for garnish

Preheat the oven to 375°F. Put 2 tablespoons of the oil, along with the vinegar and garlic cloves, into the blender; process until combined. Put the beet, carrots, and onion on a baking sheet, toss with the oil-vinegar mixture, and roast for 35 minutes, tossing halfway through, or until the beet is fork-tender. Remove from the oven and allow to cool.

Put the roasted vegetables, brown rice, oat flour, egg, cumin, and coriander in the blender container and run on medium for 10 seconds. Using a spatula, push the ingredients toward the blade and run for another 10 seconds. Add the chickpeas and pulse another one or two times, until just combined. Form the mixture into patties and chill for 1 hour. Put the bread crumbs on a plate and, just before frying, lightly coat each patty. To fry, heat the remaining 2 tablespoons of oil over medium-high heat in a skillet. Gently slide the patties into the pan and cook for about 3 minutes on each side or until lightly golden brown. Top with a slice of goat cheese and sprouts to serve.

Zesty Black Bean Burgers

The spicy combination of ingredients in these patties puts them somewhere between a burrito and black bean dip. Fry them up in a hot pan so they're crisp, with an interior that's soft but not mushy, and you've got a black bean burger. I like to eat them on a salad and not a bun, but either way they'll fill you up.

Serves 4–6

1 garlic clove, peeled and cut into quarters

½ small red onion, peeled and cut into quarters (about ½ cup)

1 small jalapeño, seeded and cut into quarters

¼ cup fresh cilantro leaves

1 teaspoon lime zest

½ cup blue corn tortilla chips, crushed

½ cup sweet potato (about ½ large potato), cooked and mashed

3 cups cooked black beans, or 2 (15-ounce) cans black beans, rinsed and drained

1 large egg, plus 1 large egg white

1 teaspoon ground cumin

3 tablespoons grated cheddar cheese

¼ teaspoon kosher salt

2 tablespoons extra-virgin olive oil

Put the garlic, onion, jalapeño, cilantro, zest, and tortilla chips in the blender container. Pulse on medium three or four times or until the onion and garlic are finely minced. Use a spatula to push everything toward the blade between pulses. Add the sweet potato and process for 10 seconds on medium. Add the beans, egg and egg white, cumin, cheese, and salt. Run the blender on low for 10 seconds or until combined. Use the spatula to stir

everything together. You want to retain some whole beans and *not* let the mixture turn to a smooth puree.

Line a baking sheet with waxed paper. Make eight patties using a ¹/₃-cup measure. Scoop out the mixture onto the prepared pan and press down slightly with your hand or the bottom of the measuring cup. Place the patties in the freezer for at least 30 minutes. When the patties are chilled, heat the olive oil in a large skillet over medium-high heat. Gently slide as many patties as you can fit into the pan, with a couple of inches between each patty. Cook the patties for 2 minutes on each side, flipping them very gently. Repeat by cooking them 1 more minute on each side (6 minutes total). Serve on a bed of lettuce with a spoonful of Fresh Pineapple Mango Salsa (page 59) and Simply Guac (page 60).

Quinoa & Butternut Squash Burgers

Filled with grains and veggies, these patties are soft and moist but still maintain a wonderful texture from the quinoa. The subtle hint of sage flavors these tender burgers that are smothered in melted Parmesan cheese and topped with oven-roasted onions, which makes them deeply satisfying.

Serves 4–6

½ butternut squash (about 1 pound), seeded and cut in half

1½ yellow onions, sliced

2 tablespoons extra-virgin olive oil, divided

¾ teaspoon kosher salt

1 egg

½ cup grated Parmesan cheese, plus more sliced for topping

4 fresh sage leaves

¼ teaspoon nutmeg

½ cup brown rice flour

3 cups cooked quinoa

Preheat the oven to 400°F. Place the butternut squash, cut-side up, on one half of a baking sheet and the sliced onions on the other. Drizzle with 1 tablespoon olive oil and salt. Gently toss the onions to make sure they're completely coated with oil. Spread them in a single layer on the baking sheet and bake. After about 30 minutes, just as the onions start to brown, use a spatula to remove them from the baking sheet. Reserve them for later. Bake the squash for another 15 to 25 minutes or until fork-tender (45 to 55 minutes total baking time for the squash). Remove from the oven and allow to cool.

When the squash has cooled to the touch, scoop out the insides. You should have about 1½ cups cooked squash. Reserve ¼ cup cooked onions for topping the burgers and put the rest in the blender with the squash, egg, grated Parmesan, sage leaves, nutmeg, and brown rice flour. Pulse several times until thoroughly blended.

Using a spatula, scrape the blender contents into a bowl with the cooked quinoa. Stir the mixture gently together and form into four to six large patties, depending on your preference. Preheat the oven to 350°F. Heat the remaining tablespoon of oil over medium-high heat in an oven-safe frying pan or cast-iron pan. When the oil is nice and hot, gently slide in the burgers (as many as you can fit comfortably without them crowding one another). Let the burgers cook for about 6 to 8 minutes on the stove top, flipping them halfway through. Next, with the burgers still in it, place the pan in the oven to bake for another 8 to 10 minutes.

Top with the Parmesan slices after about 7 minutes of baking time, and remove from the oven when the cheese is melted. The total cooking time is about 15 minutes. Top with the reserved oven-roasted onions and serve over a bed of dressed greens.

Spinach Chicken Enchiladas with Ancho Chile Sauce

There are several steps to making this dish. You have to make the sauce, then the filling, and finally assemble the enchiladas. You can always make the sauce a day or two in advance, or even assemble the whole dish a day or two before you're serving it. Each element is important to the whole, and truly worth the effort. This dish is always a crowd-pleaser. Please note, you can purchase a rotisserie chicken to use in this recipe, or you can poach and shred your own.

Serves 4–6

FOR THE ANCHO CHILE SAUCE

3 ancho chile pods (about 1½ ounces), stems removed and seeded

1 tablespoon extra-virgin olive oil

1 large onion (about 2 cups), coarsely chopped

2 garlic cloves, peeled and sliced

1 (32-ounce) can fire-roasted tomatoes, such as Muir Glen Organic

1 cup chicken broth

2 tablespoons balsamic vinegar

2 teaspoons Worcestershire sauce

1 tablespoon freshly squeezed lime juice

½ teaspoon ground cumin

½ teaspoon dried oregano

½ teaspoon kosher salt

⅛ teaspoon freshly ground black pepper

FOR THE FILLING

3 cups shredded cooked chicken

1 (10-ounce) package frozen chopped spinach, thawed

1 (15-ounce) can black beans, drained and rinsed

1½ cups shredded sharp cheddar cheese

1 cup fresh or frozen corn kernels

4 ounces canned green chiles

1 tablespoon lime juice

¼ cup fresh cilantro leaves

½ teaspoon kosher salt

⅛ teaspoon freshly ground pepper

FOR THE ENCHILADAS

½ cup shredded sharp cheddar cheese

12 small corn tortillas

To make the sauce: Put the chiles in a bowl and cover with boiling water. Let stand for 30 minutes, then drain, reserving both the chiles and the liquid. Heat the oil in a skillet over medium-high heat and sauté the onion and garlic for 5 to 8 minutes or until softened. Add the tomatoes and softened chiles, and cook another 10 minutes. Stir in the rest of the ingredients, cook another minute or so, and transfer the mixture to the blender along with ½ cup of the reserved chile liquid. Blend until smooth. Set aside.

To make the filling: In a large bowl, put all the ingredients for the enchilada filling. Add 1 cup of the Ancho Chile Sauce and mix together until well combined.

Preheat the oven to 350°F.

To assemble the enchiladas: Pour 1 cup of the Ancho Chile Sauce in the bottom of a 9 x 13-inch baking dish. Dip a tortilla in the sauce and fill with 3 heaping tablespoons of filling. Roll up and place seam-side down in the baking dish. Repeat with the remaining tortillas. Spoon about 1 additional cup sauce over the top of the enchiladas, top with ½ cup cheddar cheese, and bake for 20 minutes or until warmed through and the cheese topping is melted.

Caribbean Shrimp Fritters with Spicy Mayo

I'm a sucker for all things fried. I don't think I've ever turned down a piece of crispy fried calamari or deep-fried chicken. And fritters, oh man. Apple fritters, conch fritters, corn fritters—I eat 'em all. You can only imagine how high up these shrimp fritters—originally a creation of my friend Jenny—are on my list of favorites. They make a scrumptious starter, but also work well as a main course paired with some satiating sides like Asian Slaw (page 79) and Bibb Lettuce with Grapefruit Shallot Vinaigrette (page 86).

Serves 4

FOR THE CARIBBEAN SHRIMP FRITTERS

¼ cup chopped onion

1 garlic clove, peeled and cut in half

½ red pepper, seeded and cut into large chunks

1 cup raw shrimp, peeled and tails removed

2 large eggs

1 cup all-purpose flour

1 teaspoon baking powder

1 tablespoon Old Bay seasoning

½ teaspoon black pepper

¼–½ cup water

Peanut oil

FOR THE SPICY MAYO

1 cup prepared mayonnaise

2–3 tablespoons Dijon mustard

2–3 tablespoons lime juice

2 tablespoons raw honey

2–3 teaspoons Old Bay seasoning

To make the Spicy Mayo: Stir together all the ingredients in a small bowl. Set aside.

To make the fritters: Put the onion, garlic, and red pepper in the blender and pulse several times. Add the shrimp and pulse another one or two times. In a medium bowl, lightly whisk the eggs. Add the flour, baking powder, Old Bay, pepper, and ¼ cup water to make a smooth batter. Fold in the shrimp mixture. If the mixture is too thick, add a little more water. Heat several inches of peanut oil in a skillet. Drop tablespoonfuls of the batter into the oil and fry until golden brown, about 3 minutes each side, moving them around so they don't stick to the bottom of the pan. Serve warm with Spicy Mayo.

Lemon-Tarragon Chicken

The delicate flavor of the tarragon permeates the chicken when it's marinated in this lemony blend. Instead of grilling the chicken, you can roast it in a 500°F oven for 35 to 40 minutes. After removing the chicken from the marinade (save it for the sauce), blot it with a paper towel and divide it between two roasting pans. Rotate the pans several times while roasting. Finish with the reserved marinade as directed below.

Serves 4–6

½ cup extra-virgin olive oil

¼ cup tarragon vinegar

½ cup freshly squeezed lemon juice (keep the rinds)

2 garlic cloves, peeled

2 teaspoons Dijon mustard

1 teaspoon kosher salt

½ cup fresh tarragon leaves, firmly packed, plus extra for garnish

1 (4½-pound) whole chicken, cut into pieces

Put all the ingredients except the lemon rinds and chicken together in the blender container and blend for 30 seconds or until smooth. Place the chicken into a resealable plastic bag with the lemon rinds and pour in the marinade. Seal and marinate for 8 hours, or preferably overnight. Preheat your grill. Remove the chicken from the marinade (save it for the sauce) and cook it indirectly for 30 minutes (coals or gas are hot on one side of the grill, the chicken is on the other), turning as needed. Move the chicken to direct heat for the last 15 to 20 minutes of cooking time to give it good color. Watch carefully so it doesn't burn. Meanwhile, bring the leftover marinade to a boil and simmer on low for 6 minutes. Pour over the chicken before serving and garnish with fresh tarragon leaves.

Roasted Turkey Breast with Chipotle Sauce

The ubiquitous chicken breast can get a little dull week after week. I find turkey breast, with its especially flavorful meat, a welcome change at the dinner table. Topping the breast with spicy chipotle sauce certainly leaves no room for boredom.

Serves 4–6

FOR THE CHIPOTLE SAUCE

1 (7-ounce) can chipotle peppers

2 teaspoons ground cumin

3 garlic cloves, peeled

3 tablespoons extra-virgin olive oil

3 tablespoons red wine vinegar

1 teaspoon Worcestershire sauce

FOR THE TURKEY BREAST

1 (3- to 5-pound) bone-in turkey breast

¼ cup buttermilk

¼ cup water

1 avocado, pitted and peeled

½ teaspoon kosher salt

⅛ teaspoon freshly ground black pepper

To make the Chipotle Sauce: Place all the ingredients in the blender container and run on high until smooth, scraping down the sides of the blender as needed. Scrape all the sauce into a gallon-sized resealable plastic bag, reserving 3 tablespoons for the serving sauce.

To make the turkey breast: Using a sharp knife, make small slits in the turkey breast. Place it in the prepared resealable plastic bag. Seal and marinate for at least 6 hours.

Meanwhile, place the 3 tablespoons reserved Chipotle Sauce (or less if you prefer a milder sauce) in the blender with the buttermilk, water, avocado, and seasonings. Process until smooth. Refrigerate until you're ready to use it. When the turkey is finished marinating, preheat the oven to 375°F. Blot the marinade off the turkey and place it in a roasting pan. Cook for 1½ to 2 hours or until the internal temperature reaches 165 to 170°F. Allow to rest for 10 minutes before carving. Serve with the prepared Chipotle Sauce.

Spinach Pesto Sauce with Rigatoni

By no means should your use of this pesto be limited to pasta. Spread it on panini, put it in a quiche, or add it to a dip. You can also play around with the ingredients. Substitute kale for the spinach or try Romano cheese instead of Parm. And again, go easy with the blending so you preserve some texture in the sauce.

Serves 4

¼ cup pine nuts or walnuts

2½ ounces Parmesan cheese

1 garlic clove, peeled

2 cups fresh basil leaves, washed and patted dry

2 cups fresh spinach leaves, stems removed

⅔ cup extra-virgin olive oil

½ teaspoon kosher salt

1 pound dried rigatoni

1 pint cherry tomatoes, cut in half

½ pound fresh mozzarella, cut into ½-inch cubes

Put the nuts in a skillet and cook on the stovetop over medium-high heat, stirring constantly, for about 4 to 6 minutes. Set aside to cool. Meanwhile, put the Parmesan and the garlic in the blender and pulse. Add the pine nuts and pulse two more times. Add the basil, spinach, oil, and salt. Pulse until just blended. Cook the rigatoni according to the package directions and drain. Return the cooked pasta to the pot, add the tomatoes, and toss immediately with the Spinach Pesto. Stir in the fresh mozzarella. Serve warm or at room temperature.

CHAPTER SEVEN

DESSERTS

Lime Tartlets with Coconut Crusts

The coconut crusts of these tartlets are a dessert in themselves. My daughter Anna likes to eat them empty. She also likes them filled with chocolate ganache. The creamy mascarpone filling is just one of many that you can use to fill these sweet crusts. A scoop of lemon curd would do quite nicely, or perhaps even a small scoop of ice cream.

Makes 24 tartlets

2¾ cups sweetened coconut

3 large egg whites

1 teaspoon pure vanilla extract

Pinch of kosher salt

1 (8-ounce) container mascarpone cheese

3 tablespoons raw honey

1 teaspoon grated lime zest, plus more for garnish

Finely diced pineapple and papaya, whole black raspberries, or other favorite fruits, for topping

Preheat the oven to 350°F. Grease a mini muffin pan with baking spray. Put the coconut, egg whites, vanilla, and salt in the blender and run on medium for 1 minute or until thoroughly combined. Use a spatula to push the ingredients toward the blade if necessary, or until thoroughly combined. Put about 1 tablespoon of the mixture in each muffin cup; press down each one with a tart tamper, or make a small depression using your fingers. Put the pan in the oven and bake for 15 minutes, or until the crusts are just beginning to brown. Remove the crusts from the pan very soon after you take the pan out of the oven so they don't begin to stick. Next, whip the mascarpone cheese, honey, and lime zest in the blender until creamy. Fill each shell with a spoonful of the mascarpone mixture and top with a tiny amount of fruit. When all the tarts are filled and topped, sprinkle with lime zest. Chill until ready to serve.

Fudgy Gluten-Free Brownies

I know it may sound unappetizing to put black beans in brownies, but it's one of those "you have to try it to believe it" scenarios. These gluten-free brownies, with the added benefit of fiber and protein, are almost too good to be true. Go ahead, give 'em a try.

Makes 1 (9-inch) pan

8 dates, pitted

½ cup boiling water

1 (15-ounce) can black beans, drained

½ cup unsweetened cocoa powder

½ cup oat flour

2 large eggs

¼ cup coconut oil

¼ teaspoon kosher salt

1 tablespoon pure vanilla extract

⅓ cup brown rice syrup

1 teaspoon baking powder

1 teaspoon instant espresso powder

¾ cup bittersweet chocolate baking chips or chunks

Put the dates in a small bowl and cover with boiling water. Set aside to soak for 10 minutes. Preheat the oven to 350°F. Grease a 9 x 9-inch baking pan with baking spray and line it with parchment paper, leaving a 1-inch overhang on two sides. Drain the dates and add to the blender jar with all the ingredients except for the chocolate chunks and process on high for up to 2½ minutes, or until the mixture is smooth. Using a spatula, stir ½ cup of the chocolate chips into the mixture in the blender.

Pour the batter into the prepared pan and spread evenly. Sprinkle the remaining ¼ cup chocolate chips on top of the brownies. Bake for 20 to 25 minutes or until a toothpick inserted into the brownies comes out clean of batter (it may have melted chocolate from a chip on it, but you'll recognize the difference—the melted chocolate is thicker and smoother). Allow to cool and remove the brownies from the pan using the parchment to lift them. Cut into squares and serve.

Wholesome Chocolate Mousse

Another covert dessert, this creamy mousse features a base of avocados for a good dose of potassium and fiber. Not what you'd expect from a rich chocolaty treat.

Serves 6

5 dates, pitted

½ cup boiling water

¼ cup chocolate chips

¼ cup almond milk

2 ripe avocados, pitted and peeled

½ cup unsweetened cocoa powder

2 tablespoons maple syrup

1 teaspoon instant coffee

2 teaspoons pure vanilla extract

Pinch of kosher salt

Put the dates in a small bowl and cover with boiling water. Set aside to soak for 10 minutes. Meanwhile melt the chocolate chips in a double boiler. Stir until completely melted. Set aside to cool. After the dates have soaked, drain them and put them in the blender and pulse several times. Add the almond milk, avocados, cocoa powder, maple syrup, coffee, vanilla, salt, and cooled chocolate chips. Blend until smooth. Spoon the mixture into small 4-ounce ramekins and chill for at least 2 hours.

Chai Tea Cake

An infusion of aromatic spiced black tea gives this cake a subtle hint of cinnamon, cardamom, ginger, and clove. The moist, fragrant cake keeps well, and can be made a day or two in advance. The creamy frosting, also infused with chai tea, ensures every bite is flavorful.

Serves 12

1 cup (2 sticks) unsalted butter

2 tablespoons (about 6–7 tea bags) chai tea

3 large eggs, at room temperature

1¾ cups organic cane sugar

½ cup firmly packed light brown sugar

2¼ cups all-purpose flour

1½ teaspoons baking powder

½ teaspoon kosher salt

¾ cup buttermilk

½ teaspoon pure vanilla extract

FOR THE GLAZE

1 cup firmly packed light brown sugar

¼ cup buttermilk

2 tablespoons unsalted butter

1 tablespoon chai tea

Preheat the oven to 350°F. Place the butter in a small saucepan and cook over medium-high heat until completely melted. Add the tea to the butter, reduce the heat, and simmer for 1 minute, stirring occasionally, then turn off the heat and allow the tea to steep in the butter for another 5 minutes. After the tea has steeped, pour it through a fine-mesh sieve into a small bowl or Pyrex measuring cup. Using the back of a spoon, press the bags against the strainer to

ensure all the butter goes through the strainer. Discard the tea. Measure out ¾ cup of the butter and set aside. Use the excess to grease and flour a decorative 10-cup Bundt pan.

Next, put the eggs and sugars in the blender container and blend for 20 seconds. Add the dry ingredients and pulse one or two times. Finally, add the buttermilk, vanilla, and butter; pulse two or three more times, until the mixture is just thoroughly combined. Use a rubber spatula to scrape down the sides of the container. Do not overmix. If the dry ingredients are not completely incorporated, stir a few times with the spatula.

Pour the batter into the prepared pan and bake for 40 to 50 minutes, or until a toothpick inserted into the center of the cake comes out clean. If the top of the cake starts to become a dark brown color after 40 minutes of baking, but the center is not yet set, cover the cake with foil while it finishes baking. Let the cake cool in the Bundt pan for 15 minutes; then turn it out onto a rack set over waxed paper to cool for 1 hour. Meanwhile, make the brown sugar glaze: Place the brown sugar, buttermilk, butter, and chai tea in a saucepan and cook over medium heat, stirring constantly, until the sugar has dissolved and the mixture just begins to boil. Remove from the heat and slowly drizzle the glaze over the cake, allowing it to run down the sides. Alternatively, skip the glaze and dust the cake with confectioners' sugar before serving.

Chocolate Coffee Quinoa Cookies

Along with its many other attributes, the blender works well as a spice and coffee grinder. Whole beans are ground in seconds by blender blades. Here ground coffee is added to a quinoa cookie with melty chocolate chips for a winning combination.

Makes 2½ dozen

¾ cup coconut oil, melted

¾ cup firmly packed dark brown sugar

2 large eggs

⅓ cup almond butter

1 tablespoon pure vanilla extract

1¾ cups quinoa flour

½ teaspoon baking soda

½ teaspoon baking powder

½ teaspoon kosher salt

1 cup old-fashioned rolled oats

1 cup bittersweet chocolate chips

3 tablespoons ground coffee beans

Preheat the oven to 350 degrees. Line two baking sheets with parchment paper. Put the coconut oil, brown sugar, eggs, almond butter and vanilla extract in the blender jar and process on medium for 20 seconds. Add the quinoa flour, baking soda and powder, and salt. Run on medium for 5 seconds then increase the speed to high for 15 to 20 more seconds or until just combined. Use a spatula to scrape down the sides as needed. Next, stir in the oats, chocolate chips, and ground coffee. Using a tablespoon measure, scoop mounds of dough onto the prepared baking sheet about 2 inches apart. Bake for 8 minutes. Allow the cookies to cool on the baking sheet for 5 minutes before transferring them to a wire rack.

Easy Whipped Cream

Literally, you can have lush heavenly whipped cream in under 2 minutes using the blender (that is, if you have all your ingredients readily on hand . . . it could take you longer to maneuver the vanilla out of the back of the cupboard!). Before my blender infatuation, I always turned to my stand mixer for whipping cream. I never even considered my tall, trusty friend. (I have yet to give it a name; it's still just my reliable unfailing Blender.) Well, folks, Blender does the job, and quite nicely I might say. No splattering cream. No waiting around. It's done before you can even think too much about it. Give it a whirl.

Makes 1½ cups

1½ cups cold heavy cream

1 tablespoon confectioners' sugar

1 teaspoon pure vanilla extract

Put the cream in the blender jar and process on medium for 20 seconds. Turn the power to high and blend for another 20 seconds. Add the sugar and vanilla and blend on high until the cream is thick and fluffy and will hold soft peaks. Push the ingredients toward the blade with a spatula if necessary to ensure that the cream blends evenly. Serve immediately.

Roasted Strawberry Ice Cream

It may seem counterintuitive to roast something that's being put into ice cream, but there's actually good reason. Roasting strawberries intensifies their flavor, and because the sugars begin to caramelize, it prevents the fruit from freezing rock-solid when blended into ice cream. Serve this with a few fresh berries on the side.

Makes about 1 quart

1 quart strawberries, hulled and cut in half

1 tablespoon organic cane sugar

1 (14-ounce) can sweetened condensed milk

1 cup whole milk

½ teaspoon pure vanilla extract

Preheat the oven to 375°F. Place the strawberries cut-side down on a parchment-lined baking sheet. Sprinkle with the cane sugar and roast for 25 minutes. Allow the strawberries to cool, then cover them and place the baking sheet in the freezer. Once the berries are completely frozen, put them in the blender and add both milks and the vanilla. Pulse several times. Transfer the mixture to a plastic container and refreeze, or freeze in an ice cream maker according to the manufacturer's instructions.

Just Bananas Ice Cream

Could dessert get any easier than this? Inspired by Eve Schaub, the author of A Year of No Sugar *(Sourcebooks, 2014), this dessert is, as the name implies, just bananas. Eve and her family embarked on a year without sugar, which she writes about so entertainingly in the aforementioned book. Frozen banana ice cream was one of the desserts they savored during that time.*

Makes 2½ cups

6 bananas

Cut the bananas into 1-inch-thick slices and spread in a single layer on a parchment-lined baking sheet. Freeze for several hours or until frozen through. Put all the frozen bananas in the blender container and run on medium until the mixture just becomes smooth. The bananas will first become crumbly, then will start to become smooth. It takes a few minutes, and you'll need to press the mixture toward the blade using a spatula several times.

If the amount seems too much for your machine, divide the bananas in half and blend. Running your blender on low also helps process the bananas. Be careful not to overwork your machine during the process. Serve immediately or refreeze if the mixture becomes too soft when blending. Top banana ice cream with ground nutmeg or cinnamon, granola, or toasted coconut.

Cherrylicious Frozen Yogurt

This is one of those recipes where the beauty of the blender is especially apparent. Dessert in seconds, literally. You can eat this creamy cherry-yogurt combination straight from the blender, or put it in an ice cream maker for a slightly firmer texture. You can also switch up the fruits. Try other frozen berries and replace the almond extract with vanilla.

Makes about 1 quart

1 pound sweet cherries, pitted and frozen (about 3½ cups)

1½ cups Greek yogurt

¼ cup raw honey

1 teaspoon almond extract

Place all the ingredients in the blender and run for about 20 seconds. Eat immediately, freeze in an ice cream maker according to the manufacturer's instructions, or place in the freezer to firm up.

Sweet Peach Ice Cream with Glazed Pecans

Fresh peaches are the star here, with supporting roles played by the maple syrup, cinnamon, and pecans, which could take the lead given the chance.

Makes about 1 quart

FOR THE ICE CREAM

1 pound fresh peaches, peeled, cut into pieces, and frozen

4 egg yolks

1 cup coconut milk

2 tablespoons maple syrup

½ teaspoon ground cinnamon

FOR THE GLAZED PECANS

2 tablespoons unsalted butter

1 tablespoon dark brown sugar

1 cup pecan halves

½ teaspoon cinnamon

Pinch of kosher salt

To make the ice cream: Put all the ingredients in the blender and run on medium for about 20 seconds. Transfer the mixture to a plastic container and refreeze, or freeze in an ice cream maker according to the manufacturer's instructions. To prepare the nuts: Preheat the oven to 350°F. Melt the butter and brown sugar in a skillet over medium heat. Add the pecans and cook, stirring constantly, for about 3 minutes. Transfer the pecans to a parchment-lined baking sheet, spreading them evenly. Bake for 5 minutes or until golden brown. Cool completely, sprinkle on the ice cream, and enjoy!

Acknowledgments

This book emerged out of a lunch between two sixth graders one winter day—Susie and Camilla, who love to bake—and their moms, one with a belief in blenders, and the other who loves to blend. Girls, thanks for including us moms.

I'd like to extend a huge thank-you to my diligent and discerning testers: Janet Balletto, Sarah Brainard, Linda Dubilier, Michele Funccius Roszko, Jennifer Hall, Jennie Hartman, Charlotte Haukedal, Camilla Kampevold, Joanne Konrath, Babs Mansfield, Amoreena O'Bryon, Michelle Perreault-Dougherty, and Kaia Smithback. Your feedback is priceless.

I would also like to thank Marcey Brownstein for kindly loaning me her beautiful kitchenware, and Peter Appelson for supplying me with gorgeous surfaces (and beloved set of silverware!). I would also like to acknowledge Migliorelli Farmstand for its outstanding produce and good-natured spirit. Thanks also to Eve Schaub for inspiring me to eat less sugar.

To Maya, Seiya, and Julia for drinking milk, all kinds, again and again!

I am especially grateful to Kyle and Nile for their enthusiastic taste testing and recipe-naming efforts.

I would also like to give a special shout-out to Peter Bosch, who did what friends do: you helped me out in a time of need.

I am forever indebted to Michael and Judith Rosenthal for graciously opening their doors, literally, even when they weren't home. I am so grateful the stars have brought us together in our cherished locale. And I'll be forever thankful to the Reisses, whose friendship and generosity I deeply treasure.

I thank my mom and dad for their endless support, for allowing me to experiment in the kitchen when I was young, and showing me by example the value of family and meals shared together.

I am also grateful to my sister Lisa, for her willingness to test and make a mess, which is so unlike her, and letting me blend endlessly at the beach. A tremendous thanks to my entire extended family who taste-tested repeatedly while on vacation—even little Henrik, who tried the soup.

I'd like to extend a big thanks to the Countryman Press team, including Michael Levatino, Anne Somlyo, and to Sarah Bennett, for all she does.

An especially huge thanks to Ann Treistman for her blender vision. You amaze me with your insight, passion, and thoroughness; not really sure how you do all you do—and you're such a pleasure to work with.

I am forever indebted to my star agent, Sharon Bowers, for her exceptional guidance. I adore you for many things, including your wicked sense of humor.

Annie Kamin, I truly appreciate that you stepped in and did what it takes to get things done—many thanks. Nina Weithorn, I am wowed by your culinary knowledge, hard work, and enchanting smile.

And to the profoundly talented Justin Lanier, who was my collaborator and partner in crime. You know I will always carry a special place in my heart for you. I thank you for making my vision a reality with your skill and determination. And an infinite amount of thanks goes to my family, who stood by me every step (or whir) along the way. To my brilliant and beautiful girls Anna and Camilla: I thank you for your willingness to try all things blended, to model and help on set, and to care—for others and the world around you. And I thank my dearest Jim for his unconditional love, support, and wit. I admire you greatly. You make my heart smile 24/7.

Index